# MEXICO
## the people

### Bobbie Kalman

**A Bobbie Kalman Book**
The Lands, Peoples, and Cultures Series

Crabtree Publishing Company
www.crabtreebooks.com

# The Lands, Peoples, and Cultures Series

## Created by Bobbie Kalman

## For Kathy Middleton

**Written by**
Bobbie Kalman

**Coordinating editor**
Ellen Rodger

**Editor**
Jane Lewis

**Contributing editors**
Kate Calder
Carrie Gleason

**Editors/first edition**
Tammy Everts
David Schimpky
Janine Schaub
Petrina Gentile

**Production coordinator**
Rose Gowsell

**Design and production**
Text Etc.

**Separations and film**
Quadratone Graphics Ltd.

**Printer**
Worzalla Publishing Company

**Special thanks to:** Jürgen Bavoni, Canadian
International Development Agency, Monique Dineis,
Antonia de Sousa-Schields, Irene Herrera, Library of
Congress, Anne McLean, Pueblito Canada, Laurie
Taylor, and Pierre Vachon

**Photographs**
Jürgen Bavoni: p. 15 (top), 17 (bottom), 18 (bottom);
Jim Bryant: p. 13 (bottom), 14 (bottom), 25 (bottom
left); Milt & Joan Mann/Cameramann Int'l., Ltd.:
p. 11 (top), 12 (bottom), 18 (top), 20 (top), 21 (top),
28, 29; CIDA/David Barbour: p. 25 (bottom right);
Betty Crowell: p. 11 (bottom), 12 (top), 22, 23 (bottom),
24, 26; Richard Emblin: p. 13 (top); Hollenbeck
Photography: p. 8 (bottom), 9 (top right, bottom),
10, 15 (bottom), 20 (bottom), 21 (bottom), 25 (top);
Wolfgang Kaehler: title page, 23 (top); Carl Purcell:
p. 9 (top left); Graeme Sheffield: p. 8 (top); other
images by Digital Stock

Every effort has been made to obtain the appropriate credit
and full copyright clearance for all images in this book. Any
oversights, despite Crabtree's greatest precautions, will be
corrected in future editions.

**Illustrations**
Antoinette "Cookie" DeBiasi: p. 30, 31
Scott Mooney: p. 4–7, icons
David Wysotski, Allure Illustrations: back cover

**Title page:** The majority of Mexican people have
both Native Mexican and Spanish ancestors. This
background reflects the complex history of Mexico.

**Icon:** sombrero

**Back cover:** The chihuahua is a type of small dog
that was once kept by the native peoples of Mexico.

**Published by**
Crabtree Publishing Company

PMB 16A
350 Fifth Avenue
Suite 3308
New York
N.Y. 10118

612 Welland Avenue
St. Catharines
Ontario, Canada
L2M 5V6

73 Lime Walk
Headington
Oxford OX3 7AD
United Kingdom

Cataloging in Publication Data
Kalman, Bobbie, 1947-
    Mexico. The people / Bobbie Kalman. - Rev. ed.
    p. cm. -- (The lands, peoples, and cultures series)
    Includes index.
    ISBN 0-7787-9362-1 (RLB) -- ISBN 0-7787-9730-9 (pbk.)
    1. Mexico -- Social life and customs--Juvenile literature. 2.
Mexico--Social conditions--Juvenile literature. 3. Mexico--
Economic conditions--1970---Juvenile literature. [1. Mexico--
Social life and customs.] I. Title. II. Series.

F1208.5 .K33 2002
972.08'3--dc21

                                              2001028191
                                              LC

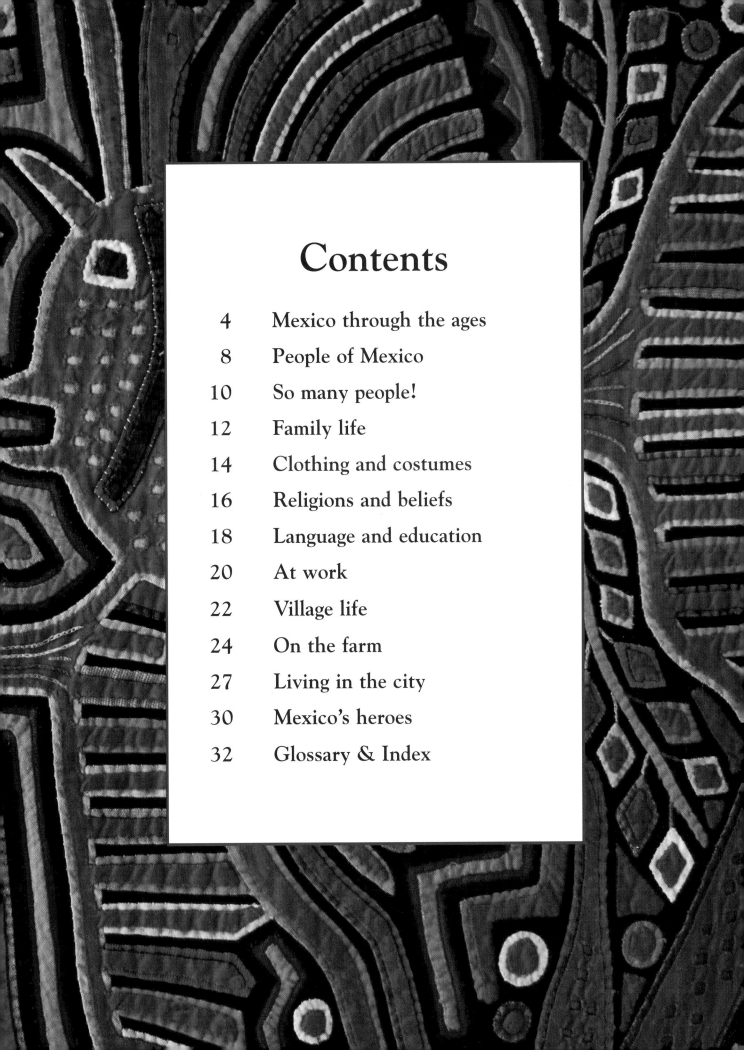

# Contents

The history of Mexico's people goes back thousands of years. The first inhabitants of Mexico were native peoples such as the Olmecs, Zapotecs, Maya, and Aztecs. These groups of people developed into advanced societies, or **civilizations**, that accomplished a great deal in the areas of arts and sciences. In the sixteenth century, the Spanish crossed the Atlantic ocean from Europe. They invaded Mexico and ruled the country for three hundred years. The people who live in Mexico today are descendants of all these different groups.

## The Olmecs

The Olmecs were the first great civilization in Mexico. They established many cities along the eastern coast and exchanged goods with other groups of native peoples. Their religious beliefs focused on a mysterious god that was part human and part jaguar.

## Teotihuacán

From 200 A.D. to 900 A.D., a great city called Teotihuacán existed in central Mexico. About 200,000 people lived there during its peak. Teotihuacán was a powerful center and controlled a large part of southern Mexico and Central America. The city was also an important religious center. Many of the gods worshiped in Teotihuacán were adopted by later peoples such as the Aztecs. Today, experts do not know what the residents of Teotihuacán called themselves. The name was never recorded, nor was it remembered by the people who followed.

*Zapotec tablet*
**600 B.C.–800 A.D.**

*Quetzalcoatl carving in a Teotihuacán temple*
**200 A.D.–900 A.D.**

*Olmec stone carving*
**1500 B.C.–200 B.C.**

## The Zapotecs

Large cities, filled with temples and pyramids, were built across southern Mexico by the Zapotec civilization. Although they were fierce warriors, the Zapotecs had an advanced culture. They studied **astronomy** and developed the first writing system in the Americas. Using **hieroglyphs**, the Zapotecs recorded their history on stone tablets.

## The amazing Maya

Around the time of Teotihuacán, the Mayan civilization had spread across southern Mexico and Central America. The Maya recorded their history, built majestic cities, and were expert astronomers and mathematicians. Food, tools, and other goods were traded back and forth between Mayan cities.

The Mayan civilization declined around 900 A.D. The large cities were abandoned. No one knows for certain why this great civilization declined. Some experts believe that hurricanes, earthquakes, disease, or war may have been responsible.

## Aztec civilization

Around 1300 A.D., another great civilization emerged in central Mexico. The Aztecs were powerful warriors who conquered neighboring peoples. The capital of their empire was the city of Tenochtitlán. This amazing city featured bridges, **canals**, and huge pyramids.

*Aztec sun god*
**1325 A.D.–1500 A.D.**

*Mayan pyramid*
**200 B.C.–900 A.D.**

## The Spanish

The Aztec civilization lasted until Spanish explorers, led by Hernán Cortés, came to America in 1519. The Spanish altered the Mexican way of life. They conquered the native civilizations and introduced European beliefs and culture to Mexico's people. For nearly 300 years, the country was controlled by Spain. During this time, the Spanish rulers gained great wealth. They found silver and gold mines, and forced the **indigenous people** to work as slaves. Millions of native people died from diseases, such as smallpox, that were brought from Europe by the Spanish.

## Dictator Díaz

The years between 1867 and 1910 were free from war. During much of this time, Mexico was ruled by a **dictator** named Porfirio Díaz. He allowed wealthy Mexicans and **foreign investors** to control Mexico's economy. Huge ranches, sometimes up to fifteen million acres (six million hectares) in size, were run by rich land barons. During this time, the Mexican peasants were overworked, underpaid, and forced to live in terrible conditions. They had no opportunity to improve their lives because all the good land was owned by the wealthy.

Porfirio Díaz
1867

Spanish ships
1519

Revolution!
1810

## Independence

In 1810, the Mexican people rose up against their rulers. The leader of this **revolution** was a priest named Father Hidalgo. Although he was captured and executed in 1811, Hidalgo is considered the father of modern Mexico. In 1821, the revolution ended and Mexico was finally free from Spanish rule.

## Years of turmoil

The next few decades were filled with war and turmoil. In 1836, the Mexican province of Texas declared independence. In a war with the United States, which lasted from 1846 to 1848, other northern territories were lost as well. A French invasion in 1863 resulted in French control for the next four years.

## Revolution

Poor living conditions led to a revolution in 1910, in which peasants fought to gain land. The **civil war** lasted for ten years and took the lives of over one million people. The country was devastated by the long and bloody war, and took almost twenty years to fully recover. Conditions did improve for the people of Mexico. A new system of government was set in place and land was redistributed more fairly. New schools were built and workers were given more rights.

*Pancho Villa, civil war hero 1910*

*Zapatista fighter 1994*

## Southern unrest

The benefits gained in the 1910 revolution did not reach everyone in Mexico. Although the country was peaceful for many years after the revolution, some people were still unhappy about the treatment of Native Mexicans. In the 1990s, a group of peasants and farmers in the state of Chiapas started another revolt. Members of this group are called the Zapatistas, after one of the heroes of the 1910 revolution— Emiliano Zapata. The Zapatistas are fighting for the rights of people living in poverty and native people in Chiapas.

*President Fox 2000*

## Mexico today

Modern Mexico is run by a central government located in the capital, Mexico City. The head of the country is the president, who is elected every six years. The **congress** creates and passes laws. There are many political parties in Mexico. One party, the Institutional Revolutionary Party, controlled the government for 71 years. This changed in the year 2000 when Mexican citizens elected Vicente Fox of the National Action Party as their president.

Each year on October 12, Mexicans celebrate their mixture of people, race, and culture in a holiday called the Day of the Race. People may have different **ancestry**, but they all consider themselves Mexican first.

## Mixed ancestry

Hundreds of years ago, native people inhabited the land that is now Mexico. When Spanish settlers came, many of them married native people. Today, six out of ten Mexicans have mixed native and Spanish ancestry. Some people with this background have dark skin, others have fair complexions.

During the seventeenth and eighteenth centuries, African slaves were brought to work on Mexican **plantations**. Many Mexicans and Africans married. Their descendants form only a small part of Mexico's population, but they celebrate the Day of the Race with pride.

## Criollos

Hundreds of years ago, the term *criollos* referred to the descendants of the Spanish people who first arrived in Mexico. Now, *criollo* is the name given to Mexico's tiny population of **caucasian** Europeans, Americans, and Canadians.

## Native Mexicans

There are over seven million native people living in Mexico today. There are more than 50 Native Mexican groups in Mexico, each with its own language and traditions. The largest groups are the Maya of the southwest, the Nahua of central Mexico, and the Zapotecs and Mixtecs of the south. Many Native Mexicans live in poverty. They rarely own the land they farm, and few are educated enough to get well-paying jobs. The native peoples of Mexico struggle to maintain their traditional lifestyles in today's modern society. Native poverty is particularly high in the southern state of Chiapas. The native people of Chiapas also face racism and discrimination from other ethnic groups.

*(opposite page, this page) Modern Mexican people come from many different backgrounds. Six out of ten Mexicans have mixed Spanish and native ancestry. There are also Mexicans with African, American, European, and Canadian ancestry.*

# So many people!

Mexico has a population of over one hundred million people, and it is growing at a rapid rate. In recent decades, many Mexicans have moved from the countryside to the cities, looking for a better life. Today, less than one-third of Mexico's people live on small farms in the country. The cities are growing quickly, but there are not enough homes, schools, and hospitals to meet the needs of every city dweller.

## A country of young people

Mexico is a country of young people—one out of every three Mexicans is under fifteen years old! It is difficult for families to support so many children. Some young people must quit school to help their parents. Farm children toil long hours in the fields, whereas city children take odd jobs to earn money. Working children have many responsibilities at a young age.

## Street children

There are as many as two million homeless Mexican children who live on city streets. Many are orphans whose only families are gangs of other street youths. Few street children have the opportunity to go to school. Without an education, their lives are not likely to improve. Some charities are trying to help these children, but their numbers are growing along with Mexico's population.

*(above) One-third of Mexico's population is under the age of fifteen.*

## The rich and the poor

Mexico is a wealthy country with valuable natural resources. Unfortunately, this wealth does not belong to everyone. A small number of Mexicans are extremely rich, and more than half of the country's citizens are poor. Many people do not have jobs, and many more have jobs that pay low wages. Poverty is particularly high in **rural** areas.

## Illegal immigration

There are not enough jobs to employ everyone in Mexico. Many Mexicans look to the United States as a place where they can earn a living. Thousands apply for legal **immigrant** status each year, but few are accepted. As a result, many choose to sneak across the border and become illegal immigrants. These Mexicans work illegally at low-paying jobs in the United States. Many workers send part of their wages home to their families in Mexico.

Illegal immigration is a source of conflict between the United States and Mexico. The American government patrols the border and arrests thousands of illegal immigrants each year. These people are sent back to Mexico, but many try again.

*(above) The number of homeless children in Mexico is growing. Charitable organizations help by creating schools for street children.*

*(below) Mexico's wealthy citizens live in expensive homes in neighborhoods such as this one.*

11

# Family life

Most Mexican families are large and close knit. The average household consists of a father, mother, two or three children, and perhaps aunts, uncles, and grandparents. Family members are loyal and supportive. They often give one another food and shelter in times of need. The most important social events for Mexicans are those involving family, such as weddings and birthdays. These are opportunities for families and friends to gather together for a **fiesta**!

## Eating together

Mealtimes are important family occasions. Family members share stories and talk with one another during their main meal of the day—the *comida*. The *comida* is eaten at 2 o'clock in the afternoon. A meal might include **enchiladas**, **guacamole**, *fríjoles refritos* (refried beans), coffee, and a delicious custard **flan**. After the *comida*, the family has a *siesta*, or rest.

## Mexican children

A new baby is a cause for celebration in most Mexican families. Parents feel fortunate and proud to have children. Mexican children tend to be happy and well behaved. They are taught to be polite, respect their elders, and work together for the good of the family. Mexican parents use a combination of firm discipline and love in raising their children.

*(top) Large families are an important part of Mexican culture, and the birth of a baby is a cause for celebration.*

*(left) The afternoon meal, called the comida, is a time of day for families to share stories.*

## Coming of age

Mexican girls look forward to their fifteenth birthday. On this day, a young girl becomes a *quinceanera*, or a *señorita*—a young woman. This celebration of entering the adult world carries many privileges. A *quinceanera* is entitled to more privacy and a later bedtime. In small towns, a *quinceanera* gains permission to join the **promenade** of young people around the town square on Sunday evenings. Many families celebrate a girl's fifteenth birthday with a large and festive party.

## Traditional roles

In a traditional Mexican household, the mother cooks, cleans, and looks after the health and welfare of the family, even if she has a job outside the home. The father usually makes the most money and is considered the head of the household. As Mexico begins the twenty-first century, however, traditional family roles are starting to change, especially in the cities.

## Modern changes

Before 1958, women could not vote in presidential elections. Until recently, Mexican women could not hold important positions in government and business. Sometimes, Mexican women are discriminated against in the workplace. Today, more and more women who live in cities are going to university and pursuing rewarding careers. Many wait until they are older to marry and have children. Some women in rural areas are the primary money earners for their family. They earn money by selling crafts such as pottery and handwoven blankets.

*(top) Grandparents play an important part in raising children and teaching good manners.*

*(bottom) This Native Mexican mother carries her baby in a large shawl in the traditional manner.*

13

# Clothing and costumes

Most Mexicans wear T-shirts and jeans, skirts and blouses, and pants and jackets. In rural areas, however, many Native Mexicans still wear traditional clothing. Festival days are occasions for dressing in colorful costumes.

## Native clothing

The clothing worn by native peoples today is similar to the clothing worn by native peoples hundreds of years ago. Traditional native clothing is made of handwoven cloth of cotton or wool and **embroidered** with colorful designs and patterns. The designs may be shapes of people, animals, plants, or mythical symbols. Some garments take months to decorate. Clothing styles and decorations differ among the many different native groups, and reflect the regions in which they live.

## Women's traditional clothing

Women wear a *huipile*, which is a sacklike white cotton dress trimmed with brightly colored embroidered flowers. An *enredo* is a wraparound skirt worn under the *huipile*. It is kept in place with a colorful waist sash called a *faja*. A *quechequemitl* is a shoulder cape with an opening for the head. This garment is worn by women in central and northern Mexico. Blouses were introduced to Native Mexicans by Spanish settlers. They are often beautifully decorated. In some areas they are worn instead of the *huipile*.

*(left) Women often wrap a shawl, called a rebozo, around their shoulders.*

## Men's traditional clothing

Traditional men's clothing has incorporated both Spanish and native styles. Men wear baggy pants, called *calzones,* that hang just below their knees. A *guayabera,* a pale-colored loose cotton shirt, is worn with the pants. A wool *poncho,* or *sarape,* is a blanket with an opening for the head that is worn for warmth. Men also wear thick-soled sandals, called *huaraches.*

## Costumes

On fiesta days, many people wear colorful and decorative costumes. Both men and women don the costume of the *charro*—a Mexican rodeo performer who does tricks on horseback. This spectacular costume is studded with gold and silver and is topped by a large sombrero with a specially shaped brim.

*(opposite page, top) Traditional native clothing is often embroidered with colorful designs.*

*(right) Some Mexican men still wear sombreros and sarapes.*

*(below) The china poblana is the traditional dress of Mexican women worn on patriotic holidays and at fancy balls.*

## The useful sombrero

The sombrero is a large-brimmed hat traditionally worn by farmers to protect their faces from the burning sun. Sombrero styles differ from region to region. In the state of Morelos, sombreros have the famous large brims. The sombreros of the Huichol people have flat crowns, medium-sized brims, and are decorated with brightly colored feathers. **Yucatán** farmers are famous for their braided palm-leaf sombreros.

## *China poblana*

The traditional costume of Mexican women is named for a legendary princess who was famous for her generosity and good deeds. The *china poblana* consists of a full skirt decorated with sequins and beads, an embroidered short-sleeved blouse, and a silk shawl. Usually, the colors of this outfit are the colors of the Mexican flag—red, green, and white. It is worn by some women on patriotic holidays and at fancy balls.

# Religions and beliefs

The Mexican **constitution** guarantees everyone the right to follow the religion of his or her choice. Ninety percent of Mexicans are **Roman Catholic**. There are also small communities of **Jews**, **Protestants**, and people who practice traditional native beliefs. Mennonites, a Christian group that believes in **simplicity** and **pacifism**, came to Mexico over one hundred years ago to escape **religious oppression** in Europe.

## Spanish missionaries

Before Hernán Cortés arrived in Mexico, native peoples practiced their own religions, which involved worshiping many gods. After the Spanish took over the country, their **missionaries** worked to convert the native population to the Spanish religion—Roman Catholicism. Roman Catholicism is a **denomination** of Christianity, a religion which is based on the teachings of a man named Jesus Christ. Christians believe Christ was the son of God on earth. Christians believe that there is only one God.

## Mexican Catholics

Although most Mexicans belong to the Roman Catholic faith, Mexican Catholics still practice some of their native ways. This may have started with the first Spanish missionaries. In order to encourage Native Mexicans to convert to the Catholic religion, the missionaries may have altered some of their **rituals** to be similar to traditional native rituals. The result is an interesting blend of religious customs. For example, Mexican Catholics celebrate a holiday called the Day of the Dead. The rituals of this holiday are similar to celebrations held by the Aztecs. The Day of the Dead occurs at the beginning of November and is a time when Mexicans honor their ancestors.

*(below) The Spanish built hundreds of churches in Mexico so that Native Mexicans could practice the Roman Catholic religion.*

## Day of Our Lady of Guadalupe

In Mexico, December 12 is the most important Catholic holiday of the year. The Day of Our Lady of Guadalupe celebrates the vision of a Native Mexican who believed that Mary, the mother of Jesus Christ, appeared and spoke to him. On the Day of Our Lady of Guadalupe, over six million Catholics from Mexico and other countries travel to her shrine, La Villa, in Mexico City. In cities and villages around the country, Mexicans wake up early and rush to the town square. A big party will last all day and night. Colorful balloons and flags are everywhere. Parades, *mariachi* **bands**, dancing, and fireworks are part of the event.

## Native beliefs

Mexico's small native population still practice traditional religious rituals. Some Mayan groups worship ancient tribal gods called *Yuntzilobs*. Although they developed in different places, native religions and Catholicism share similarities. For example, both Catholics and Native Mexicans practice forms of **confession**, **baptism**, and **fasting**.

*(above) Mexicans have added their own flavor to Roman Catholicism. This colorfully decorated church is in the southern state of Tabasco.*

*(below) There are a small number of Mennonites living in Mexico. Mennonites lead simple, traditional lives.*

17

# Language and education

Before the 1910 revolution, Mexico had a low **literacy** rate. The revolution improved the lives of Mexico's people. Hundreds of schools were built, and millions of people learned to read and write. The government continues to promote and support the education system. Today, nine out of ten Mexicans can read and write.

## Help from the movies

Movies played an important part in helping Mexicans learn to read. Many Mexican people love to watch movies, especially American movies. In the 1950s, the Mexican government passed a law requiring all foreign movies to have subtitles rather than dubbing. This meant that instead of hearing the Spanish translations of English, the viewers had to read the Spanish words on the bottom of the screen in order to follow the story.

## School for everyone

The Mexican government provides free public education for children from ages six to fourteen. Children start *primaria,* or primary school, at age six. Primary-school children begin their school day at 8 a.m. and stay in class until 1 p.m., with a mid-morning snack break. After a late lunch, the afternoons are used for extra classes or sports. Primary school has six grades.

*(this page) Mexican students have classes in history, math, science, art, and physical education. Some schools also have a garden, which helps students learn about agriculture.*

## Little workers

All children are supposed to go to primary school for six years. Sadly, many families cannot afford to buy the books or supplies their children need to attend school. Many children quit school at an early age to work and help their families earn money. Children in towns and cities sell small items on the street to earn money. Children in the country work in their family's fields planting and harvesting crops. Some native children do not attend school because they do not speak Spanish and cannot understand the lessons.

## High school

After primary school, about half of all students go to *secundaria*, or high school, for three years. *Preparatoria*, or college preparatory school, lasts for three more years. Some high schools and college preparatory schools are privately run by the Roman Catholic church. Parents pay fees to send their children to these schools, which provide a better preparation for university. Most secondary schools and college preparatory schools are located in urban areas. Many rural children do not have the opportunity to achieve more than a primary education.

## Higher education

Mexico has more than 300 professional schools, including universities, teacher-training colleges, and technical schools. Every year, over half a million young people earn a degree or diploma. Education helps young people find jobs and allows Mexico to remain an important country in world trade and technology.

*(below) Over 100,000 students attend the National University of Mexico. Founded in 1551 by Charles V of Spain, it is the oldest university in North America.*

With such a large population, Mexico's best resource is its people. Mexican people are hard workers who often spend long hours at difficult jobs to make ends meet for their family. Unfortunately, with so many people in the country, there are not enough jobs for everyone. Large numbers of Mexicans are unemployed. Others can find only temporary or seasonal jobs.

## Agriculture

One-quarter of all Mexicans work on the land as farmers. They grow crops such as corn, wheat, tomatoes, or cotton. Some farmers raise livestock. Other people are employed in the fishing industry. They fish in the country's lakes and coastal waters, using modern and traditional methods.

*(above) A motorized bike helps this police officer navigate Mexico's busy city streets.*

*(above) One-quarter of Mexico's population work in the agricultural industry. The farm worker on this modernized farm in the Yucatán Peninsula is picking mangoes.*

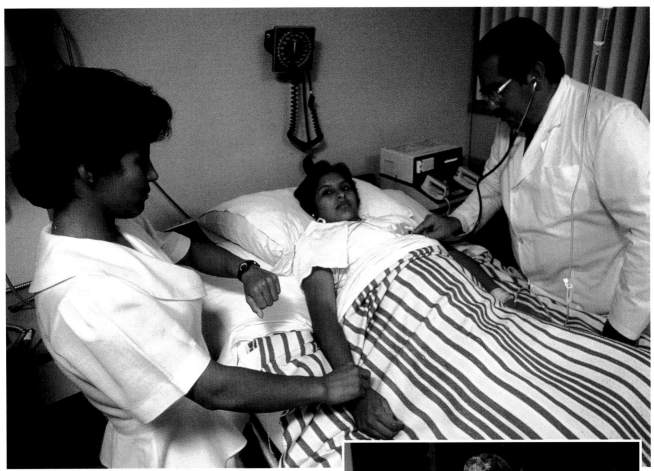

## Providing a service

About one-half of Mexican workers are employed in the service industry. Daycare providers, taxi drivers, and store clerks are service workers. Many Mexicans work for themselves as street vendors. They sell items such as snacks, drinks, blankets, jewelry, souvenirs, and clothing. The tourism industry creates many jobs for service workers. Each year more than six million tourists visit Mexico. Mexican people work in hotels, souvenir shops, and restaurants in the tourism industry.

## Factory work

About one-fifth of Mexico's workers work in large factories making goods such as cars, food products, and electrical machinery. Many factory workers work in unsafe or unhealthy conditions and make little money. Most factories are located in Mexico City or along the Mexico–United States border. These areas are full of people looking for factory work, but there are not enough jobs for everyone.

*(top) Some Mexicans have professional jobs, such as doctors, engineers, teachers, and scientists.*

*(bottom) About one-half of all Mexican workers are employed in the service industry, such as this waiter.*

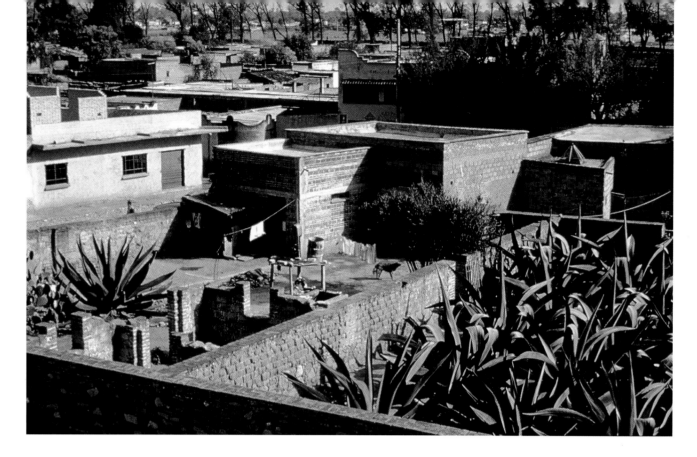

# Village life

The Mexican countryside is dotted with small villages. Many villages were established by native people hundreds of years ago. When Spanish settlers came to Mexico, they moved into the villages and built new buildings. The settlements came to resemble typical Spanish villages complete with a church and a town hall. Not all villages are alike of course, but most Mexican villages have at least two features in common—a central plaza and a marketplace.

## A place to gather

A plaza is a public square for everyone in the village to enjoy. Most plazas include a small tree-filled park paved with **flagstones** and lined with benches. The plaza is the heart of the village, where fiestas and celebrations take place. The town hall and the largest church in the village can usually be found on the border of the plaza.

## The marketplace

The marketplace is where people from the village and the surrounding farmland buy, sell, or trade goods. Vendors rent small stands or simply spread their goods out on a blanket on the ground. Most marketplaces are located near the plaza. Some are held in a large building that looks like a warehouse and others are held outside in an open area. Vendors sell everything imaginable, including fruits and vegetables, meat, dairy products, medicinal teas, electronic equipment, clothing, and traditional handicrafts.

## Market day

Bargaining, also called haggling, is an important part of doing business at the market. Haggling over a price can get very loud, but it is always considered fair business. Besides buying and selling goods, market day is a good time for friends and family to get together. The busiest day is Sunday, when local farm families flock to the village. After the market closes, people often gather in the plaza to chat with friends and listen to a band play music.

*(above) Village homes often have courtyards and gardens surrounded by brick walls.*

## The *paseo* in the plaza

The *paseo* is an old tradition still practiced in some villages. This is a time when young people meet and socialize with one another in the plaza. On Sunday evenings, teenaged girls stroll clockwise around the plaza, as boys walk counter-clockwise. If a boy wants to meet a girl, he asks her if he can walk with her. Walking together can lead to dating. Parents sit on benches or walk along the edge of the plaza keeping an eye on their sons and daughters.

## Moving to the cities

In rural areas, there is not enough land or work for everyone. Over the past 50 years, many people have moved from villages to big cities. Today, less than one-third of Mexicans live in villages. Rural areas remain some of the poorest areas in the country. Many young people have no choice but to go to the cities to find work.

*(right) The plaza is an important place for friends to socialize on Sundays after the market closes.*

*(below) Rural families look forward to the weekly visit to the market.*

# On the farm

In the early 1900s, wealthy landowners had control of the farms in Mexico. They hired peasants to farm their land and paid them very little. After the revolution in 1910, land was divided more fairly among the peasants. Many farmers worked under the *ejido* system. An *ejido* is a farm shared by several families. Each family farms a small plot of land on the *ejido* and uses or sells the crops it grows. On some *ejidos*, several families work on one large area of land and share the profits at harvest time. Farmers could not buy or sell their land, but they could pass it on to their children.

## Disappearing *ejidos*

Unfortunately, most *ejidos* are not profitable. Old equipment which the farmers cannot afford to replace and poor soil are part of the problem. In 1992, the government made it legal for farmers to buy and sell land. *Ejidos* are disappearing as

many farmers sell their farmland to large companies. The farmers either move to large cities to search for work or they stay and work on the farms as employees.

## Crops

Cotton, wheat, corn, beans, coffee, tomatoes, and tropical fruit are some of the crops grown in Mexico. Only one-fifth of Mexico's land has nutrient-rich soil and receives enough rainfall for farming. Much of the remaining land is arid, or dry. The best farmland can be found in the Central Plateau region.

*(above) Mexican farmers live in modest homes built from materials from the surrounding landscape. The roofs on these rural houses are thatched, meaning that they are made from plant stalks.*

## Praying for rain

Some farmers use **irrigation** to bring water to dry areas so that they can grow crops. Many farmers also believe that prayer can bring rainfall. The rainy season begins in late May and ends in September. If rain has not fallen by June, farm communities pray to statues of Catholic **saints** to bring rain. Some native farmers even pray to Tlaloc, an ancient rain god.

## Humble homes

In rural Mexico, three generations often live in a one- or two-room home. Some houses are built of adobe brick, which is made of dried clay. Others are built of straw. These homes have no electricity or dependable water supply. Family members sleep on straw mats called *petates*, which are spread out over hard, dirt floors. Women prepare food on a *metate*, which is a smooth stone used as a kitchen counter. Homes are cheerfully decorated with flowers and handmade crafts.

*(above) Many farms in northern Mexico are ranches, which raise livestock such as the long-horn cow shown here.*

*(left) Rural homes often do not have electricity or a dependable water supply, but are cheerfully decorated with flowers and handmade crafts.*

*(below) Most farmers lack the money to buy modern farming equipment. A great deal of work must be done by hand.*

# A day on the farm

Emiliano is a farmer in the state of Michoacán. His mother named him after Emiliano Zapata, the revolutionary leader who fought for the peasants' right to own land. Emiliano's farm is ten acres in size. In a few months he hopes to see most of it covered in corn. He and his wife Maria have two sons. Roberto, the oldest, moved to Mexico City last year to work in a factory. Emiliano is glad that Roberto was able to find a job; many of his friends' sons have not been as lucky. Emiliano's youngest son, Carlos, helps him with the farm, but he knows that Carlos will also have to leave home soon.

This morning Emiliano wakes up early to begin plowing. Carlos is taking a pig to sell at the market. Maria serves a breakfast of **tortillas**, beans, and sweet dark coffee. As Emiliano readies the oxen, he wonders whether this year's crop will be successful. Last year the rain did not come, and the crops failed. It was a hard winter, but Roberto helped by sending money home.

While her husband is plowing, Maria works hard. In the morning she makes tortillas and puts together a lunch, which she takes to Emiliano in the fields at midday. She washes the laundry by hand and hangs it to dry in the yard. In the afternoon, she tends their vegetable garden and feeds the chickens and pigs. She hopes that there will be enough money this year to send Carlos to school in the city—he wants to become a doctor.

At the end of the day, Emiliano and Carlos return home very tired. Maria has prepared tortillas with beans, pork, and tomatoes. She has added a lot of chili peppers because Emiliano likes his food spicy. In the evening Maria and Emiliano discuss the future. He would like to buy a new horse this year, but Maria convinces him that saving for Carlos's future is more important. They go to bed early, falling asleep to the sound of crickets chirping in the fields.

*(below) Carlos uses a team of oxen to plow a field.*

 Living in the city

Nearly 80 percent of Mexico's population live in big cities. The country's three largest cities are Mexico City, with a population of twenty million, Guadalajara with five million, and Monterrey with three million citizens. City life in Mexico is much less traditional than village life. Many people live in apartments and work in office buildings. Like other modern cities in North America, Mexican cities have skyscrapers, sports stadiums, parks, and fancy restaurants. They also have poverty stricken areas, heavy pollution, and traffic problems.

## Air pollution

Air pollution is so thick in Mexico's major cities that sometimes it is difficult to breathe. Smog often looks like a thick fog hovering over the buildings. Mexico City is one of the most polluted cities in the world. The pollution is caused by the factories around the city and the millions of cars that clog the city streets. Each year, thousands of people get sick because of the pollution.

## Too many cars!

Mexico's cities have too many cars and not enough roads! Traffic jams often make driving a car downtown slower than walking. Street vendors weave through block after block of idling cars, selling motorists everything from newspapers to on-the-spot car washes.

*(above) Millions of vehicles in Mexican cities cause traffic jams and pollution.*

27

## Traveling underground

Mexico began building its first **subway** system in Mexico City in the 1960s. While digging the subway, workers at the Piño Suárez station discovered the ruins of an Aztec temple. Now Piño Suárez is not just a subway station—it is also a mini-museum! Today, trains on the underground Métro whisk people across the city quickly and inexpensively. Millions of people travel on the subway every day. Guadalajara also has a subway system.

## Life of luxury

Most wealthy Mexicans live in cities. Some live in luxurious apartments and others own large houses. Their modern homes have television sets, satellite dishes, and swimming pools. Servants look after their children, clean their homes, and tend their gardens.

## The middle class

There is little affordable housing in Mexico's larger cities, so many middle-class Mexicans live in smaller cities. Some of these cities were originally Spanish **colonial** towns in which houses were built around central courtyards. Several families share a courtyard. These homes have balconies and decorative archways. Some houses are divided into apartments, allowing several families to live under the same roof. They share washing and cooking facilities.

## Slums and shanties

Every major city in Mexico is surrounded by low-grade housing. These poor areas are known as shantytowns. The shantytown around Mexico City is home to millions of people and covers hundreds of acres. Pollution, crime, and unsanitary conditions are major problems in shantytowns. The poorest people do not even have shelter. At night, homeless people cover themselves with their *serapes* and huddle together in doorways.

*(below) Shantytown houses are made of planks, plastic sheeting, and tin. Thousands of these makeshift homes surround Mexico's big cities.*

# A day in the city

"Buenos días, Juanita," calls Juanita's mother from her bedroom door. It is 6:30 a.m. and time for Juanita to get up for another day.

"Sí, mama," says Juanita sleepily. She climbs out of bed and gets washed and dressed for school. She wears her school uniform—a plaid, pleated skirt, a white blouse, green sweater, and socks.

Juanita lives in a three-room apartment on the ground floor of a small apartment building. She lives with her mother, father, grandmother, and two younger brothers, named Ramon and Antonio, or Tonio for short.

Last month, her Uncle Eduardo also came to live with them. He moved to the city from the small town in the country where he grew up. Uncle Eduardo will live with Juanita's family until he can find a job and support himself.

*(below) Juanita and her school friends trade snacks in the schoolyard*

After breakfast, Juanita helps clear the dishes and says good-bye to her family. Everyone has a busy day ahead of them. Juanita's mother is off to her job in a factory where she assembles radio parts. Her father leaves to open his barber shop with Uncle Eduardo, who has a job for the day helping a delivery man.

"Hurry up, slow poke!" yells Juanita as Tonio scrambles to catch up behind her. Ramon is too young to go to school, so he stays home with grandmother. Juanita and Tonio walk for ten blocks, past many apartment buildings, two churches, and several street vendors, on their way to school. The streets are crowded with other people hurrying to school and work. Juanita is used to the noise of the bustling city with hundreds of cars, trucks, and buses honking and people shouting to one another.

Juanita can't wait to get to school to see her friends and go to science class, her favorite subject. When Juanita grows up she wants to be a nurse. At lunch time, she and her friend Maria talk about their favorite actors. This weekend Maria's mother is taking the girls to see a movie at a big theater downtown. They can't wait!

At 1:30 p.m., Juanita meets her brother in front of the school and they walk home together. Tonio then heads off to help their father at the barber shop. Juanita takes care of Ramon while her grandmother goes shopping. She also finishes her homework so that she can watch television after dinner.

Everyone is tired at the end of the day, but they enjoy eating dinner together. Juanita tells her family that she is writing an essay on a woman named Frida Kahlo—a famous Mexican painter. Uncle Eduardo tells a funny story about helping some men lift a broken down car onto the sidewalk so that his delivery truck could pass through a traffic jam. Juanita loves to hear her uncle talk about his adventures in the city.

# Mexico's heroes

Mexicans have a long tradition of celebrating the people they admire through songs, stories, and poems. Some heroes are important historical figures, others are artists and athletes.

## "Perish the Spaniards"

On September 16, Mexicans celebrate Independence Day and honor Father Miguel Hidalgo y Costilla. Father Hidalgo was the leader of the 1810 rebellion against the Spanish. With the **slogan** "Perish the Spaniards," Father Hidalgo led an army of 80,000 Mexicans to regain Mexico's freedom.

## The Mayor's Wife

María Josefa Ortiz de Domínguez is another hero of the 1810 rebellion. She was the wife of the mayor of Querétaro and a strong believer in Mexican independence. Risking great danger, she passed a message to Father Hidalgo, telling him that the government had heard of the planned rebellion. Knowing the authorities were coming, Father Hidalgo and his followers were able to get away. Doña Josefa's bravery is still remembered today. Her face appears on Mexican coins and paper money. Her statue, called La Corregidora, or The Mayor's Wife, stands in Mexico City.

## The Savior of Mexico

Every year on March 21, Mexicans celebrate the birthday of Benito Juárez—"the Savior of Mexico." Juárez was a Zapotec and the first native president of Mexico. From 1857 to 1872, Juárez created new laws and programs to protect human rights and help less-privileged Mexicans.

## Revolutionary heroes

When a ruthless general named Victoriano Huerta seized control of the Mexican government in 1910, the Mexican people began a civil war. Two of the most famous revolutionary leaders were Emiliano Zapata and Pancho Villa. Their slogan was "Land and Liberty" because they wanted both for the Mexican peasants. Today, Zapata and Villa are remembered in patriotic books, songs, and movies.

## An inspiring woman

In the seventeenth century, a Mexican **nun** named Sister Juana Inès de la Cruz was famous for her writing. Her poetry is considered among the finest ever written in the Spanish language. Over the last 40 years, Mexican women have fought for equal rights. Many people admire Sister Inès, who inspired Mexican women to follow their dreams.

## Sports legend

Like other North Americans, Mexicans love *béisbol*, or baseball. The first great baseball player to come from Mexico was a man named Bobby Avila. He played with the Cleveland Indians during the 1950s. Avila is a national hero. After he retired from baseball, he became an important Mexican politician. Today, Bobby Avila is a legend and role model for many young Mexicans.

## Masked heroes

In 1994, a group of people called the Zapatistas started a revolution in the southern state of Chiapas. They were led by a man called Subcomandante Marcos. He is also known as "The Lord of the Mountain," and no one knows who he really is. Marcos always wears a ski mask to hide his face. Comandante Ramona is another leader of the Zapatista movement. She also wears a mask. The Zapatistas are fighting for the rights of native people in Chiapas, many of whom are extremely poor. The people of Chiapas have no electricity, running water, or access to education and health care. The Zapatistas are fighting against large landowners who control most of the land. The army is helping the landowners, but many Mexicans support the Zapatistas' cause.

*(opposite page) For many Mexicans, Emiliano Zapata is a hero who represents the struggle for equality and dignity. Along with other revolutionaries, Zapata fought for the rights of less-privileged Mexicans.*

*(top right) Super Barrio is a hero among Mexicans young and old. He inspires Mexicans to fight for what they deserve.*

## Super Barrio

In 1985, a terrible earthquake hit Mexico City and caused the deaths of thousands of people. Many people blamed the deaths on poorly constructed buildings. On June 12, 1987, thousands of people protested low housing **standards** in front of a government building. Suddenly, fireworks exploded overhead, and a masked man appeared, wearing red tights, a long cape, and the letters "SB" on his chest.

No one knows the true identity of Super Barrio, but since 1987, many men dressed as Super Barrio have fought for the rights of the Mexican people. They campaign against pollution, poor working conditions, and the unfair treatment of women and the elderly. Super Barrio cannot fly and does not have super powers, but, for many Mexicans, he is an important symbol who stands for the power of the people.

# Glossary

**ancestry** The line of people from whom one is descended

**astronomy** The study of the stars and planets

**baptism** The ceremony that shows a person has become a Christian

**canals** Artificial rivers that link larger bodies of water

**caucasian** A person with light-colored skin

**civil war** A war that occurs between two groups within a country

**civilization** A society with a well-established culture that has existed for a long period of time

**colonial** Describing a land or people ruled by a distant country

**confession** The act of telling your sins to a priest and making amends

**congress** A government body that makes decisions and passes laws

**constitution** A document that states the laws of a country.

**denomination** A religious group within a faith

**dictator** The sole ruler of a country who holds all the power in government

**discriminate** To treat unfairly because of race, religion, or gender

**embroider** To decorate fabric with colorful needlework

**enchilada** A tortilla filled with meat or cheese

**fasting** Not eating food for a period of time

**fiesta** A lively Mexican celebration

**flagstone** A large, flat stone

**flan** A molded custard dessert topped with caramel

**foreign investor** A person or company who puts money into a nation other than their homeland

**guacamole** A dip made from avocados

**hieroglyph** A picture that represents a word or sound

**immigrant** A person who moves from one country to another

**indigenous people** The first people to live in a certain region or country

**irrigation** The process of watering crops using artificial channels or streams that run through fields

**Jews** People who follow the religion of Judaism

**literacy** The ability to read and write

***mariachi* band** A small band composed of a singer, violinist, guitarist, horn player, and bass player

**missionaries** People sent by a church to spread their religion to those who do not know or believe in it

**nun** A woman who has dedicated her life to God

**pacifism** The belief that war and violence are not good ways to solve problems

**plantation** A large farm that specializes in one type of crop

**promenade** An unhurried walk

**Protestants** Christians who believe that the Bible is the most important source of religious instructon

**religious oppression** Denying people's rights because of their beliefs

**revolution** A war in which people in a country fight against those in power

**ritual** An act performed regularly, often for religious reasons

**Roman Catholic** A branch of Christianity that is headed by the pope

**rural** Describing or relating to the countryside

**saint** A person recognized for his or her holiness

**simplicity** A system of not having items that are not needed in order to live

**slogan** A saying used by many people

**standards** Levels of quality set down as a guide or model

**subway** An underground train system

**tortilla** A flat, thin bread made from cornmeal

**Yucatán** Describing the large Mexican peninsula that juts into the Caribbean Sea

 # Index

    1 2 3 4 5 6 7 8 9 0   Printed in U.S.A.   2 1 0 9 8 7 6 5 4 3